APPROACH

APPROACH

THE
ZERO-FLUFF GUIDE
FOR THE OPENING
SECONDS OF
CONVERSATION

ERIC WAISMAN

APPROACH: The Zero-Fluff Guide for the Opening Seconds
of Conversation

Library of Congress Control Number: 2024918037

Paperback ISBN: 979-8-9912352-0-4
eBook ISBN: 979-8-9912352-1-1

Published by:
Jaunty, LLC
www.jaunty.org

To Steph, my beautiful wife
and the best approach I ever made.

CONTENTS

Introduction...1

The Direct Approach.. 5

   Strategies for Approaching a Group 11

The Indirect Approach 17

   The Art of Creating Humor............................21

   Additional Indirect Approach Strategies......................33

Overcoming Social Anxiety.................................. 41

Approach Logistics 63

   The Impact of Grooming and Fashion 65

The Power of Mood on Social Behavior 73

Body Language Mastery 83

Make Your Approach... 97

INTRODUCTION

THE ZERO-FLUFF GUIDE FOR THE OPENING SECONDS OF CONVERSATION

WELCOME TO *APPROACH*, your comprehensive guide to the art and science of saying hello to someone new.

With over 15 years of experience teaching these principles, I've refined strategies and insights that have helped thousands of people enhance their social skills and navigate their social lives. Now I'm using my knowledge to help you explore the realm of introductions and become more comfortable with meeting new people.

This book is designed to teach you how to best approach someone. The goal is to prepare you for any introduction so you can come up with a great approach on the spot, no matter what situation you're in.

So, what is the "Approach"? It is the pivotal moment when you decide to engage with another person. It's the first step in any social interaction, where you transition from being an observer to becoming an active participant in a conversation. It involves breaking the ice and setting the tone for the potential relationship that may follow. It's about demonstrating openness, interest, and respect toward the other individual, creating the right environment to set up a positive interaction.

However, it's important to note that this book focuses solely on mastering the approach—literally only the first 10 seconds or so of opening a conversation. Be forewarned: it does not go into the subsequent stages of a conversation or interaction like "what to say next" or small talk. The first 10 seconds are worth learning on their own. The book only takes you through the approach leading to asking an opening question.

Here's a simple example:

> *"Hey, I saw you pick the last few songs from the jukebox over there. Impressive choices. I think you actually just made the party twice as fun, so I had to come say hi! I'm Eric. Where'd you get the good taste in music?!"*

Simple, right? Yet, through Jaunty, the social skills platform and school we have founded, I've found it's one of the most difficult interactions that people struggle with. The goal here is to equip you with the necessary skills and confidence to successfully initiate a conversation, paving the way for further communication.

This book will illuminate different aspects of the approach, filled with real-world examples and actionable advice. We'll explore various factors that influence our ability to approach others, such as the Direct Approach, the Indirect Approach, social anxiety, your environment, the power of grooming and fashion, and the profound impact of mood on social behavior.

Whether you're a social butterfly looking to refine your skills or a quiet introvert seeking strategies to build connections, *Approach* has something to offer you. Through this enlightening journey, you will not only transform how you approach others but also gain deeper insights into your own social behaviors and perceptions.

With over a decade of experience under our belt, Jaunty.org has had the privilege of guiding more than 10,000 individuals on their journeys of social connection. Our clientele ranges from top-tier corporations in Silicon Valley (where we started) to diverse individuals worldwide.

Our expertise is not simply based on our experiences but also draws from the wealth of knowledge accumulated through hundreds of thousands of approaches. Our instructors and students have both contributed valuable insights that shape our methods.

Jaunty's journey began unofficially in 2008, five years prior to its official incorporation in 2013. This timeline reflects our enduring commitment to helping people master the art and science of social skills, and I look forward to continuing this work with *Approach*.

In this guide, I will present you with the most effective and practical approach methods. These techniques have been refined over years of hands-on experience. My aim? To empower you on your path to social growth and connection.

The skill of approaching has allowed me to build the network I needed to start a business as well as to make the fateful approach on Main St. in Santa Monica that led to a wedding with my wonderful wife and then to having my son. I hope it empowers you to take even the smallest of steps toward talking to someone new. Sometimes that's all that's required to plant the seed of a relationship.

Moreover, you are invited to join our thriving community at Jaunty.org, where you can connect with like-minded individuals, actually practice the approach in real time with others, share experiences, and continue learning beyond the pages of this book.

THE DIRECT APPROACH

THE REFRESHING POWER OF THE TRUTH

LET'S START WITH THE SIMPLEST, yet psychologically most difficult, approach.

The Direct Approach is a straightforward and effective method for initiating conversations with people you're interested in. Instead of relying on pickup lines or beating around the bush with something fancy, you express your intentions honestly. The magic lies in its simplicity and the truth it holds.

Your body language plays a big part in the Direct Approach. Open and slow body language, strong eye contact, a loud enough voice, and a smile are the best combination here.

"Hey, I saw you walking by, thought you looked cool, and wanted to say hi. I'm Eric. What have you been up to today?"

It's bold. This method of starting a conversation with someone you're interested in is as refreshing as it's effective. It's like walking into a room and turning on a light, illuminating your intentions without any shadowy pretense.

WHY CHOOSE THE DIRECT APPROACH?

Choosing the Direct Approach has its advantages, particularly in its clarity and efficiency. When you opt for this approach, you're communicating your intentions and feelings in a straightforward manner, leaving little room for ambiguity or misunderstanding. This can be especially appealing in a fast-paced world where people appreciate clear communication. It allows both parties to know exactly where they stand, which reduces the time and energy spent on deciphering indirect cues or hints.

The Direct Approach also fosters a sense of authenticity and sincerity. By openly expressing your thoughts and desires, you demonstrate a level of vulnerability and trust, which can be the foundation for a deeper and more meaningful connection. For people who value straightforwardness and transparency, the Direct Approach not only helps in establishing clear communication but also in building trust and rapport.

BREAKING DOWN THE DIRECT APPROACH

In order to effectively perform the Direct Approach, you should know what it involves.

Picture this: you're at an event, and your gaze lands on someone who piques your interest. Instead of deploying a contrived icebreaker or plotting intricate strategies, you cast aside the games and simply introduce yourself, expressing your genuine interest in getting to know them better.

"Hey, I've seen you talking to a bunch of people at this party; it looks like you know everyone! I wanted to say hi—I'm Eric. How do you know everyone here?!"

Uncomplicated, right? But oh, how powerful—and how difficult—it can be! Let's dissect the anatomy of the Direct Approach.

1. THE HELLO

Your opening move is a simple yet warm greeting to capture their attention. "Hey," you say, waiting for their eyes to meet yours before you proceed. Other greetings could be "Hello," "Excuse me," or "Hi." The key is to ensure that you're in their peripheral vision—never sneak up on them from behind. As you say this, you can tilt your head back a bit and be loud enough so they know you're talking to them, yet give them some space. Again, wait for eye contact before you move on.

Your tone should be smooth, almost as if you recognize them. Think of the tone you would use for a statement like: "Hey, are you the person who was on the show *The Office*? I love that show; I watch it all the time. Are they recording a new season of it?" It's a tone that creates context, or a good reason to be saying hi.

2. THE OBSERVATION

Here, make a remark about something you've noticed—about them, the environment, or the situation. It's an olive branch, extending a connection based on shared experience or surroundings. For instance: "I've seen you talking to a ton of people at this party. It seems like you know everyone!" This shines the light on context.

3. THE WHY

Now you reveal why you've approached them. Be sincere and clear about your intentions. "I wanted to say hi," you share, baring your intentions without a hint of aggression or pushiness. "I had to come introduce myself" and "I felt drawn to come over and say hi" are other examples. Don't pause after this—go straight into the introduction. You can add more truth in this part as well, for instance, something like: "I thought you looked cute/interesting/stylish, and I wanted to say hi." You did it! You were open and honest.

4. THE INTRODUCTION

This is where you introduce yourself. Confidence and clarity are your best friends here. "I'm Eric," you say, extending your hand for a friendly shake if they seem receptive. Remember they may say hi back and tell you their name. So be ready to add something like: "Nice to meet you, Stephanie." You officially now know each other—now try and act like it!

5. THE LEAD

Finally, you transition into the conversation or small talk, steering the conversation into more personal waters. "How do you know everyone here?" you ask. You can emphasize the word "do" in this case to tie back to your observation and why. Be ready if they take what you said and redirect the conversation somewhere else: this is a good thing. For instance, after you say, "...it looks like you know everyone! I'm Eric." They could say something like, "Well, I'd better—I paid for this party! And after all of that, I still haven't tasted the cocktails!" In that situation, you would skip your lead and go down the new path.

NOW BRING IT ALL TOGETHER

Now that we've broken it down, you'll be able to clearly recognize each part within the approach. Here's a practical example to illustrate how these five pieces fit together:

> *"Hey, I noticed you from across the room and saw you checking out the bookshelf. I'm a huge reader myself and wanted to say hi. I'm Nadia. How do you like the party so far?"*

Bear in mind that not everyone will respond positively to a Direct Approach—and that's perfectly fine. It's all part of the learning curve. When done right, the Direct Approach can be a potent tool for meeting new people and forging connections.

THE DIRECT APPROACH IN ACTION

The Direct Approach isn't for the fainthearted (although we'll discuss how to reframe your beliefs and manage your social anxiety around this a little later in the book). The Direct Approach is about seizing the moment, embracing your intentions, and boldly stating your interest or attraction. It's a powerful strategy that demands a certain level of confidence and finesse. So, muster up your courage, put on your best smile, and dive right in. Who knows where the truth could lead you?

Let's see the Direct Approach in action and delve into some real-life scenarios.

EXAMPLE 1: Picture this: You're at a coffee shop, and your eyes land on an attractive woman. You feel a pull toward her. Gathering your composure, you walk over and say, "Hey, I saw you sitting there, thought you looked cute, and wanted to say hi. My name is John. What's yours? Nice to meet you, Sandra. What have you been up to today?"

EXAMPLE 2: At a party, you spot a guy who intrigues you. You navigate through the crowd, approach him, and say, "Hey, I saw you hanging out over here enjoying your drink, and I wanted to come and say hi. I'm Rachel. What's your name? Nice to meet you, Ryan. Have you enjoyed the party so far?"

EXAMPLE 3: You're at a bar, and a group of people laughing and having a good time catch your attention. You walk over and say, "Hey, I couldn't help but notice how much fun you guys are having. I thought you looked like the most fun group here, so I had to come over and say hi. What are you all celebrating?"

In all these examples, the person approaching exudes clarity and confidence. They own their intentions and are unafraid to show vulnerability. Now let's add a dash of humor to this Direct Approach.

EXAMPLE 4: You're at a party, and you see a woman standing alone. You walk up to her and say, "Hey, I saw you over here all by yourself like me, and I figured I should come over and save us both from the boredom. My name is Mark. What do you think we can do to spice up the evening?"

Using humor not only lightens the atmosphere but also makes the other person feel at ease. It's a win-win situation: the person being approached feels flattered and amused, while the one doing the approaching effectively breaks the ice and fosters a connection. We'll learn much more about humor in the Indirect Approach section a little later on, but it can be successfully used here, too.

The Direct Approach is about building a genuine connection based on truth. In a world where people often hide behind screens and filters, this approach is a breath of fresh air.

STRATEGIES FOR APPROACHING A GROUP

The beauty of the Direct Approach lies in its versatility; you can use it in almost any situation. You can also apply it not just to individuals but also when engaging with a group. Approaching a group may seem daunting, but with the right strategies, you can confidently navigate these situations.

1. WAIT FOR OPPORTUNITIES

In group dynamics, it's crucial to identify the right moment for your approach. Look for instances when the group naturally splits or when some members break off for a moment. These moments present a less intimidating opportunity to engage with one or two individuals rather than addressing the entire group at once. This approach is less intrusive and allows for a more personal connection. It's also a good time to introduce yourself and get a feel for the group's interests and dynamics, which can make it easier to engage with the larger group later.

2. CONTEXT MATTERS

Understanding the setting and context is key when approaching a group. In certain situations, like networking events or social gatherings, it's generally acceptable and perhaps even expected to approach a group directly.

When joining a networking or business group, it's important to listen attentively to the ongoing conversation before jumping in, almost as if they reeled you in like a fish with something you heard them say. This demonstrates respect for the group's dynamic and allows you to understand the context of their discussion. When you do contribute, ensure that your input is relevant and adds value to the conversation, which will help in being received positively by the group. Just in case they look at you and wonder why you're there, you can say, "Keep going—I heard you talking about cryptocurrency, and I had to hear this."

When joining a more social group, the Direct Approach can work well if the members aren't very engaged with each other.

3. DIRECT HONESTY

Direct honesty is a powerful tool in group interactions. You can simply use the same Direct Approach in plural form. Explain in a friendly and open manner why you've approached the group, whether it's due to a shared interest, to seek information, or simply to socialize. This kind of honest communication can disarm potential skepticism and foster a sense of trust and rapport. It shows that you respect the group enough to be forthright, which can encourage members to welcome you and engage in conversation.

APPLYING THESE STRATEGIES

Sounds simple enough, right? Of course, putting these strategies into practice is easier said than done, so let's take a look at a few examples of how you can approach a group in different settings:

EXAMPLE 1: You notice a group of people discussing a topic and laughing hysterically at a networking event. You wait for a natural pause in the conversation before approaching the group.

"Hey, I saw you all laughing over here, and you looked like the most engaging group at the event. I had to come and say hi. I'm Eric. How do you all know each other?"

EXAMPLE 2: You're at a social gathering and see a group of people who seem friendly and approachable. You walk up to the group and smile.

"Hey, I saw you all having a great time, and I thought I'd come over and introduce myself. I'm Amanda. What are you guys celebrating?"

EXAMPLE 3: You're at a conference, and you see a group of people mingling after a session. A couple of people break off into a separate conversation, so you approach the smaller group.

"Hey, I've seen you both in a lot of the same sessions as me and wanted to introduce myself. I'm Jessica. What do you think of the conference so far?"

Using these strategies, you can effectively approach groups more directly. For instance, you can join a group discussing a topic you're passionate about at a networking event or approach a friendly group at a social gathering and introduce yourself.

One adjective that seems to work really well when approaching someone new is "approachable." It's pretty hard to be upset at being called "approachable" (or to reject it altogether).

> *"Hey, I saw you standing over there, and you looked really approachable, so I thought I'd come say hi. I'm Lauren."*

Speaking of rejection, I'm now going to give you an almost bulletproof type of thing to say if a group or individual is not receptive to your approach:

> *"I see. Well, I'm still glad I came over and said hi. I was drawn toward you for some reason. I hope you have a great evening."*

It's amazing how often, later on in the evening if you've been talking to other people, they seem to come back around after this.

KEY TAKEAWAYS

The Direct Approach has five parts:

1. **The Hello:** Greet the person warmly and approachably without coming across as aggressive.

2. **The Observation:** Make a remark about the person or situation, which establishes common ground.

3. **The Why:** Explain why you're approaching the person, being honest and clear about your intentions.

4. **The Introduction:** Introduce yourself confidently and clearly.

5. **The Lead:** Engage the person in small talk, probing deeper into the conversation.

TASK

Approach someone using the Direct Approach.

You can also think up Direct Approaches from situations you find yourself in daily, even if you don't actually say them all out loud. Use all five parts and imagine how you'd say them.

However, to master the art of the Direct Approach, get out there and practice! Approach at least three new people this week, track their responses, and note your anxiety levels before, during, and after the interactions. We'll be working on social anxiety a little later in the guide.

Remember, the key to a successful Direct Approach lies in confidence, clarity, and authenticity. So, step out of your comfort zone, take a deep breath, and say, "Hey..."

THE INDIRECT
APPROACH

SUBTLETY AND SMOOTH STARTERS

IN THE DANCE OF SOCIAL INTERACTIONS, mastering the art of the Indirect Approach can be a game changer. This strategy allows you to initiate conversations without appearing too direct or forceful, which adds an element of intrigue and amusement to your interactions.

Unlike the Direct Approach, which is all about getting straight to the point, the Indirect Approach employs humor, wit, and situational awareness to foster a relaxed atmosphere. It's a fun and fancy way to approach.

WHY CHOOSE THE INDIRECT APPROACH?

The allure of the Indirect Approach lies in its capacity to alleviate pressure and fear of rejection. Instead of directly expressing interest in someone—which can be intimidating—the Indirect Approach lets you gauge their interest through their response to your playful comment or question. It deflects the pressure from you to your remark, which allows you to test the waters before investing too much. When executed correctly, the Indirect Approach feels more organic, witty, and enjoyable, adding a dash of finesse compared to the straightforward Direct Approach.

The Indirect Approach is about finding common ground or context with the other person and using humor or intrigue to build rapport and establish a connection. It could be a clever comment about the environment or a humorous observation about the person's appearance or behavior.

BREAKING DOWN THE INDIRECT APPROACH

Unlike its more straightforward counterpart, the Indirect Approach isn't bound by a formula, which allows for a more fluid and adaptable style of interaction. It offers you the flexibility to seamlessly weave your introduction into the fabric of a conversation by using the environment. This can be particularly effective in social settings where the atmosphere is more relaxed and a Direct Approach might seem too forceful or out of place.

By understanding and utilizing the subtleties of the Indirect Approach, you open yourself to a realm of social interactions that are both dynamic and engaging, yet comfortably unassuming.

ADOPTING THE
"BOARD GAME APPROACH" ATTITUDE

Before we get to learning the Indirect Approach, let's work on the mindset. Imagine you're carrying a game of Monopoly at a party and you want to invite someone to play. How would you go about it?

A Direct Approach might have you walk up to them, maintain direct eye contact, and boldly say, "You seem like a fun competitor. Would you accept my invitation to play this game with me?"

Conversely, an Indirect Approach might involve casually holding up the game, looking around nonchalantly, and announcing, "I'm setting up this game over here—join in, if you dare!"

Let's delve deeper into how this works.

APPLYING DIFFERENT LEVELS OF PRESSURE WITH THE INDIRECT APPROACH

An Indirect Approach could be as simple as making an observation about the environment. For instance, if you're in an overtly red bar, you could turn to a person next to you and say, "I wonder what the owner's favorite color is." This comment doesn't pressure the person to respond, but it provides an opportunity for engagement. Also, imagine engaging in eye contact up until the word "owner's" and then looking around at the red bar while finishing the statement with a smirk—it just barely opens that door of opportunity for them to engage with you. Try acting that out.

If you wish to add a bit more pressure, you could modify it with a more obvious question or add a humorous observation: "I wonder what the owner's favorite color is—any guesses?" Or you start with "Doesn't this remind you of *The Shining*?!" These comments send a clearer invitation for interaction by turning your remark into a question.

Consider these real-life examples where you can apply the Board Game Approach Attitude:

EXAMPLE 1: At a networking event, you spot someone next to you standing alone, nursing their drink. You smile warmly, hold up your glass, and say, "I think the bartender is trying to get me drunk! Is yours this strong? Reminds me of college!"

EXAMPLE 2: At a party, you notice a group of people laughing and sharing stories. You join the circle and quip, "What did you guys drink to make you all so happy? Can I have some?" After their response, you can ask, "Seriously, what are you all celebrating?"

EXAMPLE 3: You're walking on a paved street, and a person whose shoes are making very loud noises is striding near you. You smoothly look at them and jest, "You'd make for a terrible ninja today!" You can add more pressure with: "Just try and sneak up on someone—let's see what happens!"

In each scenario, the other person has options in how they choose to react, rather than simply feeling pressured to respond to you directly. This makes the interaction feel dynamic, as they have more flexibility.

As with a Direct Approach, they can react positively (e.g., laugh, add to it, or agree), negatively (e.g., ignore you or respond rudely), or neutrally (e.g., give a noncommittal response). But their response to the Indirect Approach will be based more heavily on your statement rather than you. This technique effectively lessens the likelihood of personal rejection, making the Indirect Approach a smoother and more enjoyable way to engage in conversations.

The Indirect Approach is easier on social anxiety but harder to come up with on the spot, whereas the Direct Approach is harder on social anxiety but easier to come up with in an instant.

The way to come up with an Indirect Approach is to pay attention to the environment. Think of yourself as someone with a keen eye who sees the environment in a unique way. For instance, it may remind you of something you can make a fun connection to. Taking your environment and morphing the situation into something more interesting by using playfulness and humor is a good way to use the Indirect Approach.

THE ART OF CREATING HUMOR
FOR THE INDIRECT APPROACH

Humor is a secret ingredient that can transform a mundane approach into an engaging, enjoyable experience—especially when using the Indirect Approach. It's the trick up your sleeve that helps you connect with people, make them laugh, and leave a lasting impression.

So, how do you weave this magic? Here are several humor formulas to add a dash of creativity and lightheartedness to your next Indirect Approach.

1. MISINTERPRETATION: THE AMUSING MIX-UP

Misinterpretation humor involves playfully misconstruing something in the environment or in someone's behavior. This type of humor often involves a playful twist on what is actually happening, offering a surprising and humorous perspective that can break the ice and make interactions more memorable.

EXAMPLE 1: Suppose someone on the bus opens up a compact mirror. You could humorously interpret it as them doing drugs and respond with: "Hey, you can't do drugs on the bus! Okay fine, but you gotta share!" This formula also incorporates elements of accusation (you're accusing them of something) and misinterpretation (you're wrong about what they're doing).

EXAMPLE 2: Imagine you're at a coffee shop and someone is intently typing on their laptop. You could jokingly misinterpret their focused demeanor by saying, "Are you hacking into the mainframe? I'm impressed! Can you delete my driving ticket?"

EXAMPLE 3: At a bar, you see someone with a little black book. You can ask, "Are you going to lead the bar sermon this evening? I think we all need it here!" (The book is obviously not a Bible but looks like one.)

2. REVERSAL: THE UNEXPECTED FLIP (SARCASM)

Reversal humor relies on sarcasm and flipping the expected meaning of a situation. For instance, if it's raining heavily outside as you leave the office for lunch, you could turn to someone in the lobby and say, "Did you bring your picnic basket for lunch? Perfect day for the park!"

Or amid a heavy cluster of restaurants on one street, you could lament, "I wish there were some place to eat around here."

This technique is excellent for teasing and flirting, especially when turned into a question. For example: "We need more food options here—should I open up a restaurant on this street? Think I'll have any competition?"

This type of approach can be quick, simple, and witty, and you can rely heavily on mundane aspects of the environment.

EXAMPLE 1: Walking into an empty restaurant: "This place is packed. You made a reservation, right?" or "The food must be really good here!"

EXAMPLE 2: On a crowded train: "It's so spacious in here, isn't it? We could even play soccer."

EXAMPLE 3: During a rainstorm: "Perfect weather for sunbathing today!" or "Did you bring your suntan lotion?"

EXAMPLE 4: Seeing someone with a large pile of books: "Just a bit of light reading, I see."

3. MISGUIDED AND BLIND: ACTING UNAWARE
Misguided and blind humor comes from characters who lack self-awareness or have a skewed perception of reality. They often make decisions on the basis of incorrect assumptions or flawed logic, leading to hilarious consequences. Imagine Michael Scott from *The Office*, whose misguided leadership and lack of self-awareness are constant sources of comedy. Or add some dark humor and you have a Mr. Burns–type character from *The Simpsons*.

EXAMPLE 1: Approaching someone reading a book: "A book-worm, huh? I respect that. In fact, I'm something of a literature expert myself. Ever heard of those Choose Your Own Adventure books? Revolutionary stuff."

EXAMPLE 2: If someone is studying or discussing a complex topic like quantum physics, interject with overconfident ignorance, saying, "Quantum physics? Easy stuff! I've watched *Star Trek*, so I'm basically an expert." This approach takes a humorous spin on the idea of being confidently wrong, displaying a lack of self-awareness that is both amusing and endearing.

EXAMPLE 3: Approaching someone at a wine tasting: "Excuse me, do you know if any of these wines pair well with cheese puffs? That's the only thing I've got."

4. ACCUSATION: THE ABSURD ALLEGATION
Accusation humor revolves around a character accusing another of something improbable or ridiculous, often on the basis of flimsy or misconstrued evidence. These accusations, especially when far-fetched or unexpected, can be a gold mine of laughter.

EXAMPLE 1: You see someone admiring a huge painting in a museum. You approach them and remark, "You're totally planning on stealing that, aren't you?"

EXAMPLE 2: If somebody looks or smiles at you, you can surprise them with a smile and say: "Are you trying to seduce me? You're smooth!" This would be a more flirty approach and can humorously catch them off guard.

EXAMPLE 3: Two people at a restaurant: "Hold up, I'm calling you out—you two are secret food critics in disguise, aren't you? You look a little judgy but love food—admit it!"

5. PINNING: CREATING IMPRESSIONS WITH POSITIVE LABELS

Pinning is a playful social skill that involves attributing or labeling someone with a positive or exaggerated characteristic, essentially creating a "pin" that sticks to them in the minds of the people involved. This technique is all about highlighting a trait or unique quality in someone. It's often used in a playful and flirtatious manner to add fun and intrigue to conversations. You can use pinning to start conversations.

EXAMPLE 1: Suppose you're at a networking event and see your friend Alex, who possesses a natural talent for connecting people. You observe him effortlessly exchanging contacts and introducing people he just met to others. This is where pinning comes into play.

You could say: "Alex, you're a networking ninja! I'm going to hire you as our Chief Relationship Builder! We'll have a million clients in no time!"

This approach not only compliments Alex's interpersonal skills but also adds a layer of humor and playfulness to the conversation.

EXAMPLE 2: Imagine you're at a lively bar and strike up a conversation with a spirited woman next to you after observing her rebellious demeanor. You could say: "You're a troublemaker! I'm gonna watch out for you!"

EXAMPLE 3: Another scenario is at a team meeting. A new coworker named Sharon quickly adds up some numbers the team is throwing around. You can later say, "Wow, Sharon, that was quick back there—you're our genius! Can you go fix the federal budget now?!"

In these scenarios, the focus is on the individual's unique traits or capabilities and positioning them in a positive, fun light. This technique reinforces their self-image and makes your interactions more memorable.

But just as important, the "pin" can be used over and over again. For example, three days later in another meeting—a day before the company is set to negotiate finances with a partner company—you quip: "Let's just send Sharon in—she'll dominate them!" This works as a callback or inside joke.

6. WIND-UP: THE ART OF PULLING THEIR LEG

The "wind-up" humor formula is about leading someone into believing a fabricated story or exaggerated claim, essentially pulling their leg or "winding them up." The objective isn't to deceive but rather to create a humorous and unexpected twist that leaves the person amused.

EXAMPLE 1: Imagine you're at a local art gallery and you see someone enjoying a group of paintings. You can look at the paintings with them and say, "These are really cool paintings. I know the artist. Did you know that these are actually all scratch-and-sniff paintings? (Pause) In fact, they're also flavored, like Willy Wonka's wallpaper!" At this point, they'll probably realize you're pulling their leg, which releases the built-up tension and results in laughter. You can add a little smirk toward the end to tip them off.

EXAMPLE 2: You see someone prepping for a marathon and trying to support their knee with a brace. You can say, "When I used to run long distances, I would just down a full bottle of vodka right before the run, which numbed the pain for me. It's great for marathons!"

These examples illustrate how wind-up humor can add fun and laughter to your conversations. They demonstrate that humor isn't always about telling jokes—it can be about creating amusing scenarios and using playful exaggeration. Remember, the delivery of these lines should be done with confidence and a playful tone to ensure they're received in the right spirit.

7. UNREASONABLE REQUESTS: THE COMEDY OF ABSURDITY

In the world of humor, there's a special place for the outrageous, the absurd, and the wildly exaggerated—and that's where the comedic formula of "Unreasonable Requests" comes in. This technique involves making ludicrous demands or requests.

EXAMPLE 1: For instance, imagine you're at a park and a biker stops nearby to rest. You could turn to them and say, "Hi, I like your bike... can I have it? I don't want to walk back home three miles!" The sheer audacity and absurdity of the request, delivered with a straight face, can induce laughter.

EXAMPLE 2: Or consider a scenario where someone is barely managing a handful of items, proudly balancing everything but clearly unable to take on more. You walk up and ask, "Hey, can you hold my baby for me, just for a minute?" The situation is already chaotic, and your unreasonable request adds a touch of hilarity. Remember, you can follow up with "No, seriously, need some help?"

8. EXAGGERATION: AMPLIFYING REALITY FOR LAUGHS

Exaggeration is a tried-and-true method of inducing laughter. It involves amplifying certain aspects or characteristics to an extreme extent for comedic effect. Exaggerating the humor techniques above is the best way to ensure that the other person doesn't think you're being serious.

EXAMPLE 1: Recall the example above: "These are really cool paintings. I know the artist. Did you know that these are actually all scratch-and-sniff paintings? (Pause) In fact, they're also flavored, like Willy Wonka's wallpaper!" The flavored part is the over-the-top exaggeration. You can add a smirk here to hit the point home. The over-the-top characterization can elicit chuckles and make the conversation more engaging.

By using exaggeration, you're not just making a joke; you're also showing interest in the other person's life by engaging with what they say in a creative and amusing way. This technique is especially handy when you want to add a touch of playfulness to a conversation without straying too far from the topic at hand.

Some more examples:

1. In a cooking class, you see someone adding sprinkles to their dessert. "I love sprinkles—just add the whole bag to it!"

2. When someone has a dog, you say, "I can't date anyone with dogs, especially puppies. They're too cute to handle—I pass out just thinking about them. My cuteness tolerance is dangerously low!"

3. Observing someone at the gym lifting weights: "Wow, you must be preparing for the next *Avengers* movie. I mean, Thor who? You're clearly the new superhero in town."

4. At a coffee shop: "I don't just like coffee—I need an IV. I'm only here because it ran out."

5. In line at a show where there was clearly a lot of traffic, you can say, "I think I aged a few decades in that traffic. Did you walk here? You still look young."

6. You see someone picking up their Amazon boxes and say, "I get it! I buy so much from Amazon that they called me yesterday to see if my house can be an official warehouse for them!"

Many of these are also wind-ups. Can you spot them? Remember, the key to effective exaggeration is to keep it lighthearted and gauge the other person's reaction to ensure that they find it amusing rather than think you're serious.

9. CALLBACK HUMOR: REINFORCING SHARED LAUGHTER

Callback humor is a powerful comedic technique that involves referencing a previous joke or humorous incident from earlier in the conversation or performance. It's like an inside joke between you and others that creates a sense of camaraderie and shared experience.

EXAMPLE: For instance, if early in the evening someone spills their drink and later on that evening that same person asks their server for a napkin, you could smile and say, 'Gonna order a second drink?' The unexpected callback to the previous incident can spark laughter and a sense of shared amusement.

Think about some callbacks from the examples in the previous section. For instance, if you see that person from the earlier example at the gym again, you can ask, "How's the movie production going?"

HOW TO FIND HUMOR ON THE SPOT

Humor is like a trusty sidekick, ready to spring into action when your conversation needs a dose of levity. It's the spice that transforms ordinary encounters into memorable experiences. But how can you summon this superpower on the spot?

Let's embark on a journey to uncover the art of spontaneous humor. One way is by asking a few key questions about your environment and using them to weave witty comments into your conversations.

QUESTION 1: WHAT IS THERE A LOT OF IN THE ENVIRONMENT?

Imagine you're at a bustling coffee shop—there's a sea of laptops and people absorbed in their work. You could playfully quip, "What startup did we walk into?" or "This isn't the nature and meditation retreat we signed up for!"

In this scenario, you've taken the abundance of laptops in the environment and turned it into a humorous observation, creating a connection over a shared moment.

QUESTION 2: WHAT IS OUT OF PLACE?

Now, picture yourself at a formal gala where everyone is very dressed up. Let's say the venue doubles as a nightclub on other nights, and you see a pole-dancing pole. You might say in jest, "Don't worry—I brought dollar bills."

Here, you've seized on the incongruity of a stripper pole at a fancy event to create a playful comment, instantly lightening the atmosphere.

QUESTION 3: WHAT THINGS IN THE ENVIRONMENT REMIND YOU OF OTHER THINGS?

Say you're at a bar, and you spot an oddly shaped oval decoration that resembles a UFO and is the color of a green M&M. You could chuckle and say, "Did you know that used to be ET's shower after he went back to his planet?"

By drawing a playful connection between the decoration and a famous movie, you've injected humor into the conversation, making it more engaging.

QUESTION 4: WHAT SUCKS ABOUT THE ENVIRONMENT?

Let's transport ourselves to a never-ending line at the DMV. You could quip to others in the line, "The DMV is so therapeutic, right?"

In this case, you've taken a universally frustrating situation and turned it into a humorous comment, creating camaraderie among those enduring the same ordeal.

As you ponder these questions, remember that humor often lies in the unexpected. It's about noticing the quirks, incongruities, and peculiarities around you and using them as comedic fodder. Don't be afraid to take a lighthearted jab at the environment, others, or even yourself.

The key to mastering spontaneous humor is practice. The more you engage in these playful observations, the more natural they'll become. Soon, you'll have your own arsenal of witty comments ready to sprinkle into your conversations, making them not only enjoyable but unforgettable. So keep your eyes open and your wit sharp, and let the laughter flow!

ADDITIONAL INDIRECT APPROACH STRATEGIES

Beyond relying solely on humor, there are other ways to approach indirectly. Let's dive into three other Indirect Approaches for starting conversations.

STRAIGHT-UP SOCIAL

This method involves going straight into small talk. It's all about showing confidence and the ability to strike up a conversation with anyone, anywhere.

EXAMPLE: Imagine you're at a social event and you spot someone standing alone, checking their phone. You walk over, give a friendly smile, and say, "Hey, how's it going?" or raise your glass and say, "Cheers! How's your night?"

Some more examples:
1. "I'm excited for this seminar—are you?"
2. "Hi there, and how's the night going with you?"

ASKING THEIR OPINION

This approach is about starting a conversation by asking for someone's thoughts or views. This can be a good icebreaker, but make sure the opinion in question is relevant because it can come across as scripted if not done correctly.

> **EXAMPLE:** You're at a bookstore and you see someone browsing the thriller section, which happens to be your favorite genre. You pick up a book by a well-known author and say, "Excuse me, I see you're into thrillers, too. Have you read anything by this author? I'm trying to decide whether or not to buy this book. What do you think?"

Some more examples:

1. While waiting in line at a coffee shop, you notice someone holding a travel mug with a logo of a famous city you've visited. You could say, "I couldn't help but notice your Paris mug. I've been there and loved it. What did you think of it?"

2. During a break in a workshop or seminar, you see someone reviewing notes from the session. Approach them with "I see you're taking detailed notes on today's workshop. What's your opinion on the speaker's viewpoints?"

3. After a yoga class, while everyone is picking up their mats, you could start a conversation by asking, "That was a challenging session today, wasn't it? How long have you been practicing yoga, and what benefits have you noticed? I'm trying to get a sense of what to expect long-term."

SITUATIONAL APPROACH

This approach involves making a comment about something happening in your immediate environment. It's about being present and spontaneous.

> **EXAMPLE:** You're at a coffee shop, and the barista has just made some impressive latte art on someone's coffee. You turn to the person next to you and say, "Did you see that? I swear, the baristas here could be artists. I can barely manage not to spill my coffee, let alone create art with it!"

Some more examples:

1. In a park, you observe someone trying to take a selfie with a scenic background. You might offer, "That looks like a great shot with the sunset behind you. Do you want me to help by taking the photo for you? This place really lights up beautifully in the evenings."

2. While waiting for a concert to start, you notice the stage setup and comment to the person next to you, "Look at all those lights and speakers! I always wonder how long it takes to set all this up. Have you seen this band live before?"

3. When the bus or train suddenly stops and everyone lurches slightly, you could turn it into a lighthearted moment by saying, "Well, that was a bit of a roller coaster! I hope that's not how the entire ride will be. Are you commuting home from work, too?"

4. At a bar you see a woman wearing interesting earrings. You might say, "Your earrings remind me of those bird-like flowers in Hawaii. Have you ever seen those?"

The key to each of these approaches is authenticity. It's about find-ing a shared experience or interest and using that as a springboard for conversation. Remember, the goal isn't to impress the other person with a clever line—it's to start a genuine conversation.

KEY TAKEAWAYS

1. **Mastering the Indirect Approach:** The Indirect Approach to starting conversations offers a more subtle and relaxed alternative to the Direct Approach. By employing humor, wit, and situational awareness, you can initiate interactions in a way that feels organic and enjoyable.

2. **Alleviating Pressure and Fear of Rejection:** Unlike the Direct Approach, which can feel intimidating, the Indirect Approach allows you to gauge someone's interest through their response to your playful comments or questions. This deflects pressure from you to your remark, making conversations smoother and less daunting.

3. **Flexibility and Adaptability:** The Indirect Approach isn't bound by a strict formula, which gives you the flexibility to weave your introduction seamlessly into the conversation. By paying attention to your environment and finding common ground or context, you can initiate interactions in a dynamic and engaging way.

4. **The Power of Humor:** Humor is a secret weapon when using the Indirect Approach. It can transform mundane approaches into memorable experiences, making people laugh and leaving a lasting impression. Experiment with different humor

formulas like misinterpretation, reversal, and exaggeration to add flair to your conversations.

5. **Authenticity Is Key:** Whether you're using humor or other indirect approaches like asking for opinions or making situational comments, authenticity is crucial. The goal is to start genuine conversations by finding shared experiences or interests rather than trying to impress with clever lines.

TASKS

1. **Observation and Engagement Exercise**

   Task: Spend 30 minutes in a public setting, observing your environment.

   Action: Note unique aspects about your surroundings and consider ways to initiate conversation on the basis of your observations.

   Assignment: Start at least one conversation using an indirect comment or question related to your environment.

2. **Humor in Conversation Exercise**

   Task: Select one or two humor techniques (like Misinterpretation or Exaggeration) to use.

   Action: Incorporate these techniques into your everyday conversations throughout the week.

   Assignment: Reflect on your experiences using humor in conversation, noting what worked well and what was challenging.

3. **Role-Playing Social Scenarios Exercise**

   Task: Engage a friend or family member (or the Jaunty Gym!) to role-play common social scenarios with you.

   Action: Practice starting conversations using Indirect Approach techniques in these scenarios.

   Assignment: After each role-play, reflect on what strategies worked and what challenges arose.

Remember, the objective is to make progress, not achieve perfection. Embrace this opportunity to step out of your comfort zone, try new approaches, and learn from each experience. Engaging with the Indirect Approach will help you develop essential social skills for various settings.

OVERCOMING SOCIAL ANXIETY

A NEW APPROACH TO PERCEIVING SOCIAL FEAR

MEETING NEW PEOPLE CAN BE a challenging prospect for many of us. The nervousness, the self-doubt, the pressure to make a positive impression—it all adds up to a daunting experience. But what if there was a way to transform this experience into something more comfortable and enjoyable? In this section, we'll explore powerful strategies that can help you do just that.

Moreover, we'll delve into tackling social anxiety, one of the most common impediments to successful social interactions. Almost everyone we work with has some level of social anxiety, and much of it originates from the approaching phase. You'll learn techniques and exercises to control and manage your fears, which empowers you to approach social situations with confidence and ease.

By shifting your mindset and employing these techniques, you can turn potentially awkward or fearful encounters into smooth, relaxed, and enjoyable interactions. With relatable examples, actionable tips, and inspiring anecdotes, this section will guide you on how to reframe your approach anxiety, build meaningful relationships, and effectively manage your negative thoughts.

REFRAME: THE FRIENDS-FIRST TECHNIQUE

One of the most potent tools you can use in overcoming initial nervousness and creating a relaxed atmosphere when meeting new people is to change your frame. But what exactly do we mean by "frame"?

Think of it as the lens through which you view a situation. Your frame shapes your perspective, your thoughts, and your emotional response. Consider it like putting on a different pair of glasses that make the world appear friendlier, warmer, and more approachable. In the context of social interactions, your frame can mean the difference between feeling anxious or at ease.

Act as if you're already friends. Act as if you may already know them or have had experience with them. This is the Friends-First Technique. You may as well test out what it would be like to be friends anyway. This subtle shift in perspective can alleviate tension, boost your confidence, and foster openness, paving the way for deeper connections.

Acting as friends immediately with someone will:

1. **ESTABLISH RAPPORT QUICKLY:** Treat the other person as a friend from the get-go, and use the same humor upfront that you would with an old friend. This instant familiarity helps you build rapport and trust more swiftly. Successfully acting this way will invite them to fall into this more comfortable frame as well, inviting easier conversation.

2. **ENCOURAGE OPEN AND HONEST COMMUNICATION FROM THE GET-GO:** This friendly attitude in an introduction provides an opportunity to dive straight into a conversation while feeling as if you're already friends. Friends are more likely to have genuine, engaging conversations, so emulating this in your interactions can lead to more authentic dialogues. The idea here is to slide right into an interaction that feels as though it would only be happening between you and someone you already trust.

3. **CREATE MEMORABLE EXPERIENCES:** Interactions that include rawer emotions and personal language are more enjoyable and memorable. They increase the chances of forming long-lasting connections.

Consider this scenario: you're about to go on a first date and meet your date right outside the planned restaurant. We'll present two versions of this scenario—one where you approach the date formally, and another where you adopt the "friends-first" mindset:

VERSION 1 (FORMAL APPROACH): You think, *I'd better play it safe and formal at first.* You say, "Hi—Sarah? Hi, it's James. Nice to finally meet you in person." You reach for a handshake. "So, have you ever eaten here before? Me neither, but I hear it's really good." You might be a bit nervous and play it safe with physical distance. "Shall we go inside?"

VERSION 2 (FRIENDS-FIRST APPROACH): You think, *This person seems cool so far in our interactions, and I hope to get to know them and at least become friendly with them. Maybe it could even blossom into something more. So let's act as if we're already friends.* You say, "Hi, Sarah!" You offer her a hug. "It's great to see you. Oh my god, that was a crazy drive over here, and my Uber driver got stuck! Hahaha. You look great. I've been waiting for a fun occasion to eat here—let's go inside! How are you?"

The difference is palpable. The friends-first approach creates a warmer, more relaxed atmosphere conducive to connection and rapport.

ADOPT THE FRIENDS-FIRST TECHNIQUE

As you might be able to tell, the friends-first technique is unique and allows for an immediate friendliness. But how do you execute this approach? Here are our two best tips.

1. **Warm Greeting:** Begin with a warm greeting, such as a friendly smile or a hug (if appropriate, depending on the context of the meeting). This works to immediately make the conversation more friendly and comfortable.

2. **Engaging Conversation Starters:** Initiate a conversation on a friendly topic rather than sticking to formalities. Open up about an interesting experience or something vulnerable. The aim is to be as engaging as possible. This immediately takes the pressure off the situation.

By using these two methods, you can transform your interactions, making them more enjoyable and rewarding while reducing the impact of social anxiety.

PRACTICAL APPLICATION: "ACT AS IF" IN REAL-LIFE SCENARIOS

This falls under the psychology of "acting as if." Understanding the theory of the "act as if" approach is one thing, but seeing it in action can truly illustrate its potential. Let's explore a few relatable examples that show how this technique can be applied in various social situations.

NETWORKING EVENTS: MAKING PROFESSIONAL CONNECTIONS PERSONAL

Picture yourself at a networking event. Your goal is to make meaningful connections, but the formal business atmosphere can feel intimidating. With the "act as if" friends-first approach, you can transform these encounters into more personal and engaging interactions.

Take the case of Alex, a software developer. Instead of starting a conversation with technical jargon or business-speak, Alex adopts a friendly tone and says, "Hey, I've heard there's some impressive brainstorming happening at this event, but I can't stay away from those empanadas at the food bar! Have you tried them yet?"

This approach creates a lighthearted and welcoming atmosphere.

GROUP ACTIVITIES: FOSTERING CAMARADERIE THROUGH SHARED EXPERIENCES

Joining a new group or club can be nerve-racking. Using the "act as if" friends-first approach can help break the ice and foster camaraderie.

Consider Emily, who's attending her first photography club meeting. She introduces herself to another member by sharing a funny story about a recent photography mishap. "Hey, that's an awesome lens you have there, probably great for outdoors. Today I thought I had the perfect shot, and I was determined to do anything to get it, but I ended up just chasing a squirrel! Am I the only one that kind of stuff happens to?!"

This relatable and humorous anecdote invites others to share their experiences, creating an atmosphere of camaraderie right off the bat. This technique can also be used if you're introducing yourself to the whole group.

SOCIAL GATHERINGS: CREATING INSTANT FAMILIARITY

At parties or social gatherings, adopting the "act as if" friends-first mindset can help you mingle with ease. Picture yourself at a lively housewarming party. You spot a group engaged in an animated conversation. Instead of hesitating, you use the "act as if" friends-first technique and join the conversation, saying, "Hey, it looks way more fun over here. I was just in the kitchen, and they're talking about taxes! Save me, please!"

By playfully joining the conversation, you project confidence and openness, creating an instant sense of familiarity that can create comfort.

JOB INTERVIEWS: BRIDGING THE GAP BETWEEN INTERVIEWEE AND INTERVIEWER

Even in job interviews, the "act as if" friends-first approach can be beneficial. Imagine walking into an interview not as an outsider but as a potential team member. You greet the interviewers warmly and say, "Hi, I've been looking forward to this. I've heard such great things about the current projects. Rosa at the front desk just showed me the secret coffee stash, so I'm ready to go!"

This approach bridges the gap between interviewee and interviewer, turning what could be a nerve-racking experience into a more relaxed, conversational interaction. This example also shows why it is important to work this approach in with the peripheral people in the environment—in this case, the receptionist.

AT A SPORTS EVENT: CONNECTING THROUGH TEAM SPIRIT

Imagine you're at a sports event, cheering for your favorite team. The atmosphere is electric, and the crowd is buzzing with excitement. Seize the moment to connect with fellow fans using the "act as if" approach. High-five a fellow fan and say, "What a game, huh? They've really surprised me this year. Think they can make the playoffs?"

This gesture of camaraderie instantly bridges the gap between strangers, uniting you over a shared passion for the team.

AT A YOGA CLASS: BONDING OVER SHARED RELAXATION

At the end of a peaceful yoga class, as everyone is rolling up their mats, use the "act as if" friend-first technique to engage with your fellow yogis. Approach one of them and say, "That was a relaxing session, right? I think it's nap time! Aren't daytime naps the best?" This lighthearted comment creates a shared moment of humor and relaxation. It's not a formal introduction, but it feels like something you would say to a friend you already knew. It opens up an opportunity for a conversation about yoga, relaxation techniques, or the simple joy of napping. You can get into the formal parts later, like finding out their name, how long they have been coming here, and where they are from.

This approach can help you form connections based on shared interests and experiences in the moment.

ADDRESSING POTENTIAL CONCERNS

While the "act as if" friends-first approach can be a powerful tool, it's important to apply it authentically and respectfully. Be mindful of personal boundaries and adjust your behavior according to the other person's comfort level. Show genuine interest in their experiences and opinions, and remember that building a connection takes time. Start with light, friendly conversation and gradually delve into deeper topics as the relationship develops.

As you incorporate this technique into your approaches, you'll likely find that it becomes second nature. Practice makes perfect, and with time the friends-first approach can help you create genuine, lasting connections with those around you.

SOCIAL ANXIETY: UNDERSTANDING AND OVERCOMING IT

As we continue working on different ways to look at reframing our thoughts around meeting new people, we must address social anxiety.

Social anxiety is an inherent part of the human condition, a universal thread that binds us all. Whether you're a seasoned social butterfly or a more reserved individual, we all have our unique degrees and sensitivities to this phenomenon. It's the flutter in your stomach when you walk into a room full of strangers, the racing heartbeat when you're about to speak in public, or the hesitation and mind going blank when introducing yourself to someone new.

But here's the good news: social anxiety is not an insurmountable obstacle. It's a challenge, yes, but one that can be overcome with understanding, practice, and a little courage.

Let's navigate the complex landscape of social anxiety together. We'll explore more frames and ways of perceiving this obstacle as well as practical strategies to help you face this ubiquitous fear head-on and hopefully reduce the sting of potential rejection associated with making an approach. We'll uncover the key to transforming social anxiety from a barrier into a stepping stone toward increased confidence and enriched connections.

Let's talk about four more techniques and strategies to help with reframing social anxiety and the approach:

THE WALLET VS. STICKER SPECTRUM: By examining the spectrum of social comfort levels in various scenarios, we'll learn how to stretch our social boundaries and expand our comfort zones.

THE 50 SACRIFICES: This concept will encourage you to take risks in social situations, viewing each attempt not as a potential failure but as a necessary step toward success.

ENCAPSULATING THE STING: We'll explore techniques to minimize and contain the discomfort associated with social anxiety, transforming it from an overwhelming experience into a manageable one.

FEAR IN FRONT VS. FEAR BEHIND: By analyzing where our fear lies—in anticipation of an event or in its aftermath—we can better understand our reactions and develop effective coping strategies.

So, let's embark on this journey armed with curiosity and openness. Remember, the aim isn't to eradicate social anxiety entirely—that would be like trying to stop the tide. Instead, our goal is to learn how to surf the waves of social anxiety, using them to propel us forward rather than letting them pull us under. Let's dive in!

THE WALLET VS. STICKER SPECTRUM: EXAMINING SOCIAL ANXIETY

Imagine you're sitting in your favorite café, engrossed in a captivating book or absorbed in your own thoughts. Suddenly, someone who has piqued your interest stands up from their chair, obliviously leaving their wallet or purse behind, which had fallen on the floor. How easy or difficult would it be for you to approach them and point out their oversight?

"Hey, it seems like you dropped your wallet back there. I thought you might need that!"

For most of us, this scenario would feel relatively effortless—it's simply a duty to assist someone in need. It's worth taking a minute to ask yourself, and self-reflect, on why that may seem pretty easy.

Now, let's tweak the situation slightly. Instead of a forgotten wallet, imagine this person has an obscure sticker on their laptop. This sticker represents a niche interest or hobby, something only a select group might recognize—think along the lines of a symbol from a cult classic film. You happen to be well-versed in that film's culture. How challenging or effortless would it be for you to strike up a conversation about that sticker?

For many, this new scenario might still feel comfortable, albeit slightly more daunting than the lost wallet situation. Again, take a minute to reflect on how easy or difficult this may feel.

Context plays a significant role in how we perceive social anxiety. Let's say that sticker fell off the person's laptop the night before, and you never had the chance to see it. Suddenly, striking up a conversation becomes more intimidating, even though it's the same person. Without the specific context of the visible sticker, approaching them becomes less straightforward. This illustrates how our minds can create barriers or excuses on the basis of the presence or absence of external cues.

Continuing along this spectrum, let's consider a scenario where the sticker is more well-known but still not universally recognized. It could be a symbol from a popular TV show or a nod to a renowned artist. In this case, approaching them might feel slightly more challenging, as you might question whether they would appreciate your knowledge or share your enthusiasm. However, this challenge isn't insurmountable, and with a dose of courage you could still initiate a conversation based on mutual interest.

Finally, let's explore a situation with no specific context or external cues, similar to the situation where the sticker fell off the laptop. The person simply piques your curiosity, and you feel the urge to connect. This can be the most daunting yet exhilarating situation. It requires stepping outside your comfort zone and embracing vulnerability. But remember, the lack of context doesn't mean there's no common ground. The environment itself—the café you're both in—can serve as shared context, offering a conversational starting point. Alternatively, you can adopt the Direct Approach and express your interest candidly, saying something like: "Hi, I couldn't help but notice you, and I wanted to introduce myself. I thought you looked interesting." This may lead to uncovering many of the similarities you share.

By dissecting social anxiety, organizing it into a spectrum, and analyzing the impact of context, we can start challenging our preconceived limitations. We can identify where our comfort zones lie and expand them, one step at a time, by recognizing that there's always something around with which to initiate a conversation, whether it's a lost wallet, a niche sticker, finding humor, or the simple desire to connect with another human being.

In social scenarios you find yourself in, pay attention to the context, or lack thereof, and ask yourself where on the spectrum you think you are. Are you more on the dropped wallet side or more toward the not-so-niche sticker side? Remember, each step along the spectrum represents an opportunity for growth. Even if the conversation doesn't pan out as planned, you're still making progress and acquiring valuable skills for future interactions by identifying where on the spectrum you are at that moment and remembering that it could all just be a false perception. Embrace the journey and observe as your social confidence grows wings.

As you reflect on your comfort level when starting conversations, you may find that, a significant portion of the time, you feel at ease initiating interactions when there's a clear context or shared interest. These scenarios—where the conversation feels natural and effortless—highlight your strengths and areas of confidence. However, you might also pinpoint more challenging situations where social anxiety creeps in and starting a conversation feels daunting.

In these instances, it's crucial to remind yourself that there's always an easy context waiting to be discovered *after* saying hello. You can expect that something like the sticker topic will get uncovered at some point once you start the conversation. By taking that first step, you open the door to potential connections and shared experiences.

Approach these challenging scenarios with an open mind and the belief that within that person lies a context or common ground just waiting to be unveiled. Embrace the thrill of exploration and trust that by initiating the conversation, you're creating the opportunity for an effortless and meaningful connection to bloom.

THE 50 SACRIFICES: EMBRACING THE CURVE IN LEARNING SOCIAL MASTERY

Imagine you're learning to play a new musical scale on the guitar or piano. To truly master it, you might need to stumble through 50 imperfect attempts before the notes start to flow seamlessly. Each of these attempts, however scratchy or discordant, is a stepping stone on your path to mastery. They help you develop muscle memory, refine your technique, and bolster your confidence in your abilities.

Now, let's apply this concept to the art of approaching people and initiating conversations. Just as you would with a new musical scale, consider your first 50 approaches as necessary sacrifices, essential steps in the process of honing this social skill. By embracing such a mindset, you detach from the outcome of each individual interaction, which allows you to focus more on personal growth and improvement.

Let's be clear: the journey to approach mastery isn't an easy one. It's essential to be raw and honest about the learning curve you're likely to face. The first few dozen attempts may feel awkward, uncomfortable, and perhaps even discouraging. Yet, it's crucial to remember that every attempt, regardless of the outcome, is a valuable learning experience.

During these initial attempts, you may stumble over your words, face rejection, or encounter other unexpected challenges. However, it's important to recognize that these experiences are an integral part of the learning process. Just as a musician must practice diligently and face setbacks to improve, so too must you persevere through the challenges of your social journey.

Ironically, as you focus on those initial 50 approaches as sacrifices for learning and growth, something remarkable happens.

As you practice, refine your skills, and embrace the learning process, you'll likely find that you're not just improving your ability to approach and converse with others. You're also making friends, landing dates, and forming business relationships along the way, even from those first 50!

ENCAPSULATION: MANAGING THE STING OF REJECTION

Rejection can leave deep scars on our emotional landscape, eroding our self-esteem and casting a long shadow over our sense of self-worth. It's a painful experience that can make us feel unworthy and question our value. However, if we encounter similar types of rejection repeatedly, it can serve as a signal, pointing us toward areas where we may need to improve.

The trick lies in encapsulating that rejection within its specific context, without allowing it to seep into our broader sense of self. Just as a single college rejection doesn't foreclose the possibility of earning a degree or pursuing a successful career, a social rejection doesn't imply a lifetime of loneliness.

THE MAGNIFYING EFFECT OF REJECTION

Imagine this scenario: a man musters the courage to approach a woman he finds attractive. He strikes up a conversation, hoping to establish a connection. Unfortunately, she politely declines his advances. In that moment, his self-esteem takes a hit. He starts doubting his attractiveness and desirability, and he fears a future of perpetual loneliness. As these thoughts spiral out of control, he begins to question his ability to find a life partner, his chances of starting a family, and even his worth as a person.

This example illustrates how rejection can be internalized and magnified, transforming a single event into a sweeping judgment of our overall worth. It's crucial to understand that these thoughts and feelings are not reflections of reality—they're distorted perceptions fueled by the emotional impact of rejection.

PUTTING REJECTION IN ITS PLACE THROUGH ENCAPSULATION

Encapsulation is a powerful tool for countering the pervasive influence and ripple effect of rejection on our self-worth. This technique involves confining the rejection event to its specific context and time frame, which prevents it from infiltrating and adversely affecting our overall sense of self.

When we encapsulate rejection, we recognize it as a temporary setback—not a commentary on our total worth. This perspective helps us prevent rejection from becoming a reflection of our core value. Establishing this mental and emotional boundary is crucial for developing a healthier response to rejection.

VISUALIZING ENCAPSULATION: CONTAINING THE SHOCK WAVES OF REJECTION

Picture your identity and self-worth as a series of concentric circles. Each circle represents a different aspect of your life—relationships, career, hobbies, personal values—with your core worth at the center, defining who you are.

Now imagine a rejection event occurring at the outer edge

of these circles. This event sends shockwaves rippling inward, threatening to disrupt and damage every aspect of your identity.

Here's where the power of encapsulation comes into play. Instead of letting those shock waves spread unchecked, visualize creating a protective barrier around the rejection event. This barrier stops the shock waves, preventing them from reaching the inner circles of your identity and self-worth. It's like a white blood cell globbing and encasing a threat. Or you can picture a bomb squad's detonation chamber containing the shock waves of a bomb to keep them from traveling outward.

By doing this, you acknowledge that the rejection is an isolated incident, not something that defines your entire existence. It's like erecting a shield to protect your sense of self from the potentially damaging effects of rejection. While the concept of encapsulation can be applied differently in other fields, the underlying principle remains the same—confining something within its specific context to minimize its broader impact.

So, the next time you face rejection, try visualizing a barrier to contain its shock waves. This will equip you better to handle rejection without letting it negatively impact your overall sense of self-worth.

FEAR IN FRONT VS. BEHIND: HARNESSING THE POWER OF PERSPECTIVE

Imagine standing at a crossroads, with two paths stretched out. Picture the path in front of you, where you must run past a family of three snakes, terrified, to reach an adventurous city. It symbol- izes the brief but difficult discomfort (pain) of facing fears and embracing vulnerability, with each step forward punctuated by moments of resilience. On the other hand, the path behind you looks like a comfortable beach, you're confined to the beach alone, and the sand is a very slow sandpit, deceptive and suffocating. It rep- resents the gradual sinking feeling of missed opportunities and stagnant comfort, where every moment spent in hesitation sinks you deeper into the quagmire of regret.

These two paths represent different kinds of pain. The pain in front of you—an approach—is immediate but fleeting. It's the nervous flutter in your stomach as you walk up to a stranger, the dryness in your throat as you say hello for the first time. It's acute and intense—but it's also momentary. Once the initial interac- tion is over, so is the pain.

Behind you, however, lurks a different kind of pain. It's a slow, gnawing pain that erodes your spirit over time—the pain of loneli- ness and "what if." This pain doesn't come in intense bursts like the fear of approach. Instead, it's a constant companion, a dull ache that never really goes away. It's the pain of missed opportunities, of looking back on your life with regret, knowing you let your fear of rejection prevent you from forming meaningful connections.

By reframing your perspective, you can harness the power of these fears to fuel your growth. Recognize, during each approach opportunity, that the fear behind you—loneliness—is far more potent and damaging than the fear that lies ahead—approach anxiety. Use this understanding to propel yourself forward toward the short-lived discomfort of initiating a conversation, rather than retreating into the long-term pain of isolation.

Remember, the temporary discomfort of nervousness pales in comparison to the long-term agony of loneliness and missed oppor- tunities. So, the next time you find yourself hesitating to approach someone new, remind yourself what's at stake. Ask your- self this: "Would I rather endure the momentary sting of starting a conversa- tion or the lasting pain of regret?

KEY TAKEAWAYS

1. **Social Anxiety Is Common:** Understand that social anxiety is a universal experience that affects people to varying degrees, regardless of their social prowess.

2. **Overcoming Social Anxiety Is Possible:** With understanding, practice, and courage, social anxiety can be overcome. It's not an insurmountable obstacle but rather a challenge to be managed.

3. **Techniques and Strategies for Overcoming Social Anxiety**

   o **The Wallet vs. Sticker Spectrum:** Recognize the role of context and external cues in social interactions, and challenge preconceived limitations.

   o **The 50 Sacrifices:** Embrace the learning curve by viewing each social interaction as an opportunity for growth, regardless of the outcome.

   o **Encapsulation:** Learn to contain the discomfort of rejection within its specific context, preventing it from affecting your overall self-worth.

- ○ **Fear In Front vs. Fear Behind:** Understand the difference between the acute fear of approach and the lingering fear of missed opportunities, and use this perspective to propel yourself forward.

4. **Embrace the Journey:** Approach social anxiety with curiosity, openness, and a willingness to explore. Each step toward overcoming social anxiety is a step toward increased confidence and enriched connections.

5. **Progress over Perfection:** Recognize that progress in overcoming social anxiety is incremental. Celebrate each step forward and learn from each experience, regardless of the outcome.

6. **You're Not Alone:** Remember that many people struggle with social anxiety. Seeking support from others can be beneficial on your journey to overcoming it.

TASKS

1. **Reflection Exercise**
   - ○ **Task:** Dedicate three minutes daily for intro-spection, recalling when social anxiety affected you that day.
   - ○ **Action:** Write down situations where you felt socially anxious, identifying patterns or triggers.
   - ○ **Assignment:** Discuss your findings with some-one you trust for insights and support.

2. **Exposure Therapy Exercise**
   - ○ **Task:** List situations that trigger your social anxiety.
   - ○ **Action:** Slowly expose yourself to these situa-tions, starting with the least intimidating. Face your fears and use the Jaunty Gym community for your support system.
   - ○ **Assignment:** Keep a journal of your experi-ences and progress with exposure therapy.

3. **Relaxation Techniques Exercise**
   - ○ **Task:** Add mindfulness exercises to your daily routine.
   - ○ **Action:** Use deep breathing, muscle relaxation, or guided meditation to manage anxious feelings.
   - ○ **Assignment:** Find which techniques work best for you and make them a daily habit.

4. Thought Challenge Exercise

- ○ **Task:** Take note of negative thoughts during social situations.

- ○ **Action:** Question these thoughts and replace them with balanced, realistic ones.

- ○ **Assignment:** Maintain a thought journal and practice reframing negative thoughts.

APPROACH
LOGISTICS

FINDING YOUR TRIBE IN
THE URBAN JUNGLE

A VERY IMPORTANT FACTOR that's often overlooked when building a social circle is your location. Navigating social landscapes can be especially difficult if you have been inside that bubble for a long while. You're usually not able to fairly compare it to other locations.

An often overlooked large element that significantly influences this journey is the city you live in. Every city pulses with its unique rhythm, which is shaped by cultural dynamics and demographic diversity.

Consider New York City, with its electrifying energy, sky-high ambition, and relentless pace. It's a magnet for individuals who thrive under pressure and relish swift, decisive conversations. Contrast this with Kyoto, Japan, a place where tranquility, politeness, and respect for tradition reign supreme, and you begin to see how different cities attract different people.

Finding your tribe isn't as simple as "just be yourself and put yourself out there." While this advice has merit, it fails to consider the influence of location on social connections.

For example, a tech entrepreneur might struggle to find investors in Lexington, Kentucky—a city renowned for horse racing and bourbon distilleries, not tech startups. Similarly, someone seeking a family-oriented spouse may face challenges in San Francisco, a city known for its analytical nature and singles culture. Demographics vary wildly as well—things like sex, age, race, sexual orientation, and religion.

This doesn't mean it's impossible to find your desired connections in these cities. It just means you may have to work harder or think creatively about where your tribe might gather. So, what do you do?

One top solution is to relocate to a city where your tribe is more likely to congregate. If you're a tech entrepreneur, consider the Bay Area, New York, or even Austin—the global hubs for high-tech innovation and venture capital. If you're seeking a family-oriented partner, a city like Provo, Utah, known for its family-friendly culture and community values, might be a safe bet.

Of course, relocation is a significant decision and is not always feasible. But understanding the cultural landscape of your city and identifying niches where your tribe might gather can go a long way toward boosting your social connections. Still, it's a good idea to move to (or visit often) where you have the highest probability.

Before diving into the social depths of a new city, identify the kind of people you want to connect with. This goes beyond shared interests to include factors like age, sex, race, and professional background. Research local culture, observe public spaces, experiment with different approaches, and adjust as needed. I can't count the number of students we've had who have found their future spouse within the first three months of moving. The social skills had been learned, but the location needed to change. Most of these examples moved out of the Bay Area to places like Los Angeles, Raleigh, and Nashville.

In the end, remember that finding your tribe involves more than honing your social skills. It's also about positioning yourself in an environment where your tribe naturally congregates. Don't be afraid to explore new cities, understand their cultural landscapes, and make a move if necessary. After all, your tribe is out there, waiting to welcome you. You just need to know where to look.

THE IMPACT OF GROOMING AND FASHION

MASTERING THE ART OF APPEARANCE FOR WINNING APPROACHES

FIRST IMPRESSIONS ARE OFTEN FORMED WITHIN A FEW SECONDS, and they are heavily influenced by our appearance—our grooming habits, fashion choices, and overall presentation. This is why it's crucial to pay attention to how we present ourselves when approaching and meeting new people.

In this section, we'll delve into the psychology and sociology behind grooming and appearance, providing practical tips and insights to help you boost your confidence and navigate social situations more effectively.

THE PSYCHOLOGY AND SOCIOLOGY
OF GROOMING AND APPEARANCE

Our appearance does more than just make us look good—it sends out signals about who we are.

From a sociological perspective, our appearance can indicate our social status, cultural background, and personal values, subtly shaping the dynamics of our interactions. It can reflect societal norms and expectations, influencing how we are viewed by others. For example, well-groomed and physically in-shape individuals are perceived as more competent, trustworthy, and attractive. This perception often leads to positive first impressions, which can be critical in social contexts.

Whether we recognize it or not, our physical fitness, grooming, and fashion choices often act as nonverbal communication tools, conveying messages about our personality, lifestyle, and even our beliefs and affiliations to those around us. In this way, grooming and appearance serve as a complex interplay of self-expression, societal norms, and psychological cues.

Just as important is how grooming and appearance impact us personally. How we present ourselves can significantly influence our self-esteem and confidence, positively impacting our interactions and overall demeanor. When we feel good about our appearance, we tend to be more open and engaging in social settings, which makes it easier to connect with others. Taking pride in our appearance can signal to others that we value both ourselves and the situations we are in, thereby fostering respect and positive interactions in our social circles.

When we understand the power of personal presentation, we can use it to help us navigate social landscapes with greater ease and bolster our self-image and confidence. Ultimately, the way we choose to present ourselves is a reflection of our inner selves and can be a key factor in shaping the quality of our interactions and relationships.

GROOMING AND SELF-CARE TIPS

Building good grooming habits is the first step in maintaining your appearance. With these tips, you can significantly enhance your self-confidence and social success.

HAIRSTYLES: Find a hairstyle that suits your face shape and personal style. Regularly visit a trusted hairstylist to keep your look fresh and updated.

SKINCARE: Develop a skincare routine tailored to your skin type, addressing specific concerns like acne or dryness.

GROOMING TOOLS: Invest in quality grooming tools, like razors, trimmers, and brushes, to help maintain a polished appearance.

HYGIENE: Ensure that you maintain proper hygiene by showering regularly, brushing and flossing your teeth, and using deodorant.

CLOTHING CHOICES FOR DIFFERENT SOCIAL SCENARIOS

What you wear can also significantly impact the impression you make on others. Dress appropriately for the occasion, keeping in mind the context and dress code.

CASUAL OUTINGS: Opt for comfortable yet stylish clothing that reflects your personality.

FORMAL EVENTS: Choose sophisticated attire like suits or evening gowns to convey respect for the occasion.

PROFESSIONAL SETTINGS: Dress professionally according to your workplace's standards, prioritizing neatness and modesty.

EVERY OCCASION: No matter where you're going, make sure things fit well! Properly fitting clothes not only enhance your appearance but also boost your comfort and confidence.

PRO TIP: Shoes can make all the difference. Investing a bit more to have cleaner and higher-quality shoes may have a larger impact than other clothing.

FRAGRANCES AND SCENTS

Scents can evoke powerful emotions and memories, subtly influencing others' perceptions of us. Experiment with different soaps, perfumes, deodorants, or colognes until you find a signature scent that complements your personality and style. The power of scent lies in its ability to create a lasting impression, often on a subconscious level, thereby playing a key role in social interactions and personal branding. A good goal if you don't know where to start is to focus on smelling clean with scents of fresh spring soap or fresh laundry.

DEVELOPING PERSONAL STYLE

To cultivate a unique personal style, explore various fashion elements and see how they align with your personality and desired social outcomes. Look for inspiration in fashion icons, magazines, and social media platforms, embracing the diverse range of styles they offer. Remember, personal style is dynamic; it can change as you grow and encounter new experiences. Don't hesitate to update your style to reflect your growth, ensuring that your style choices continue to resonate with who you are and who you aspire to be. Your fashion can also lead to deeper conversations. For instance, if you bought a unique bracelet on a trip, it can enhance your storytelling by sharing about it if someone asks.

INVEST IN YOUR APPEARANCE

Investing in your grooming and fashion choices is an essential aspect of improving social confidence and making good impressions. This also includes having a physique that raises your confidence, or at least doesn't bring it down. Embrace the journey, experiment with different looks, and discover what works best for you.

- Try approaching people sporting different looks, hairstyles, clothing styles, and fragrances.
- Try trimming, shaving, or waxing different parts of your body.
- Invest in a fitness trainer or classes.
- Buy shoes with different heel sizes that can make you taller.

- Talk to a dermatologist about your skin.
- Keep track of people's reactions and interactions to understand the impact of grooming and appearance on social outcomes.

Remember, your grooming choices and appearance reflect your personality. When you feel confident in how you're presenting yourself, you're better equipped to tackle social challenges and build stronger initial bonds with people.

KEY TAKEAWAYS

1. **The Power of Appearance:** Recognize that first impressions are greatly shaped by grooming habits, fashion sense, and overall presentation.

2. **Confidence Boost:** Acknowledge how good grooming significantly affects self-esteem and confidence, positively influencing your demeanor and interactions.

3. **Personal Style Investment:** Dedicate time and effort to crafting a unique personal style that aligns with your personality and social aspirations.

4. **Try New Things:** Be open to experimenting with various hairstyles, clothing styles, scents, and grooming routines to discover what suits you best.

5. **Learning by Observation:** Pay attention to people's reactions when you experiment with different looks to understand how grooming and appearance influence social outcomes.

TASKS

1. **Self-Evaluation:** Evaluate your current grooming and appearance choices. Identify areas where you can improve to better reflect your desired image.

2. **Exploration and Study:** Spend time exploring different fashion styles, grooming habits, and cultural norms related to appearance. Try incorporating elements into your style that resonate with you.

3. **Tailored Grooming Routine:** Create a personalized grooming routine that caters to your skin type, hair texture, and personal preferences. Stick to this routine consistently to maintain a well-groomed appearance.

4. **Seek Feedback:** Ask friends, family members, or mentors for feedback on your grooming and appearance choices. Use their insights constructively to refine your style.

Remember, enhancing your grooming and appearance is a continuous journey. Enjoy the process, stay open to trying new things, and aim to present the best version of yourself to the world.

THE POWER OF MOOD ON SOCIAL BEHAVIOR

MOOD IS AN OFTEN OVERLOOKED yet powerful influencer in our social interactions. Whether you're on cloud nine or under the weather, your mood significantly affects your approachability and ability to connect with others.

This section will delve into the importance of mood in social situations and provide practical strategies to help you leverage positive moods, understand mood influencers, and warm up for successful social engagements.

THE RIPPLE EFFECT OF MOOD ON SOCIAL INTERACTIONS

Our mood serves as a filter through which we view the world, subtly shaping our perceptions and actions. But it doesn't just affect us—it also ripples outward, influencing those around us. Not many people pay attention to their mood before meeting new people, mostly because they are too self-conscious about how they look or what to say.

When we're in a positive mood, we're likely to come across as more approachable, open, and engaging, attracting others to us like a magnet. This can lead to more meaningful connections and open doors to new opportunities.

Conversely, a negative mood can cast a shadow over our interactions, creating invisible barriers that hinder connection or turn people off. It can inadvertently communicate discomfort or disinterest, even when unintended, which may lead others to misconstrue our intentions or feelings.

Being mindful of our emotional state and its impact on our social environment can make or break the start of a healthy and rewarding relationship via an approach.

THE POWER OF "SOCIAL MOOD"

"Social mood" is a concept referring to a mental and emotional state that enhances our social skills and makes us more adept at navigating social situations. It's characterized by feelings of energy, confidence, and genuine interest in others.

Activating this "social mood" involves tapping into a mindset where positivity, open-mindedness, and empathy are at the forefront. When we are in this state, our body language becomes more inviting, our conversations are more engaging, and our ability to read and respond to social cues sharpens.

This heightened state of social awareness not only helps in creating a favorable impression but also in building deeper, more authentic relationships. It's about aligning our internal emotional state with our external social interactions, thereby enriching every social encounter we engage in.

By identifying and harnessing this state, we can improve our ability to approach new people and foster meaningful connections.

BOOSTING YOUR MOOD
FOR THE LONG TERM

Achieving a positive mood isn't always about waiting for the stars to align—it's something we can actively cultivate. Here are some strategies:

SLEEP: Implement a consistent sleep schedule to ensure that you're well-rested and alert. Adequate sleep improves cognitive function and emotional regulation, making it easier to maintain a positive outlook.

DIET: Embrace a balanced diet rich in whole foods, providing your brain with essential nutrients for mental well-being. Avoid processed foods and unhealthy ingredients.

EXERCISE: Regular physical activity can act as a natural mood booster, reducing stress and promoting feelings of happiness. Exercise also releases endorphins, known as "feel-good" hormones, which can elevate your mood and energy levels.

ENVIRONMENT: Create a positive environment filled with uplifting sights, sounds, and smells. Sunshine and nature are great environments. Personalizing your space with items that bring joy or relaxation can significantly enhance your daily mood and productivity. Reducing plastics, distancing yourself from cell towers and radiation, and surrounding yourself with people you love are other great aims for your environment.

MENTAL WELL-BEING: Practice mindfulness, meditation, or other stress management techniques to maintain a balanced mental state. Limit screen time and artificial light. Something we focus on at Jaunty is creating a positive social circle in our lives and avoiding people who don't want the best for us. These practices help in cultivating a sense of inner peace and resilience, which are essential for navigating life's ups and downs.

NAVIGATING EXTERNAL FACTORS

External factors, such as weather and environment, can also sway your mood and social behavior. It's important to recognize these influences and adapt accordingly.

For instance, on gloomy, rainy days, when your energy might be lower, opt for cozy indoor activities. These can be comforting and can provide a more intimate setting for social interactions.

Conversely, sunny weather often brings an increase in energy and positivity, making it the perfect opportunity for outdoor social events. Embrace the outdoors on clear days to elevate your mood and encourage more active and engaging social interactions.

In addition to the weather, the change of seasons and cultural events can also impact our social mood and activities. Embracing seasonal activities, like attending a summer festival or a winter market, aligns us with communal rhythms and can open up new avenues for socializing and enjoying shared experiences.

Being aware of and responsive to these external factors allows us to harmonize our social life with the environment, leveraging the unique opportunities each setting presents for enriching our social interactions and overall mood.

BOOSTING YOUR MOOD FOR
THE SHORT TERM: WARMING UP

Just as athletes warm up before a game, warming up both physically and mentally before social interactions can enhance performance. Here are some tips to get you in the right state of mind for a successful interaction.

VOCAL WARM-UPS: Loosen up your vocal cords with exercises to ensure clear, confident speech. This not only improves your articulation but also helps in managing your tone and pitch, making your communication more effective.

ENERGIZING ACTIVITIES: Boost your energy and mood with activities like dancing, singing, or brisk walking. These activities increase your heart rate and release endorphins, which naturally elevate your mood and prepare you for social engagement.

MENTAL PREPARATION: Visualize successful social interactions, rehearse conversation starters, and celebrate your strengths. This mental rehearsal can reduce anxiety and increase your confidence, helping you be more adept at handling various social situations.

SUPPLEMENTS: Certain supplements or enhancers can boost your mood immediately. This includes coffee, for instance. Experiment to find the right amount and when to ingest it in order to ensure that it complements rather than disrupts your natural rhythm.

PRACTICING SOCIAL INTERACTIONS

Practicing social interactions can be fun, enhance your mood, build confidence, and refine your skills.

ROLE-PLAYING: Play out various social scenarios with a friend, taking turns to approach each other and respond to different topics.

ONLINE TOOLS: Use random sentence generators to practice responding to unexpected statements.

SIMULATED SCENARIOS: Gradually increase the difficulty level in your practice sessions, mimicking real-life social settings and challenges.

Understanding and leveraging the power of mood in social interactions is key to overcoming social anxiety and enhancing communication skills. By adopting mood-boosting strategies, warming up before social encounters and practicing with various tools and techniques, you can elevate your ability to approach new people by feeling more sociable and motivated.

KEY TAKEAWAYS

1. **Influence of Mood:** Acknowledge that emotions play a significant role in social interactions, affecting how approachable we are and how we connect with others.

2. **Positive vs. Negative Emotions:** Recognize how positive emotions foster openness and engagement, while negative emotions can pose obstacles to forming connections.

3. **External Variables:** Stay aware of external elements like weather and environment that have an impact on mood and adjust your social behaviors accordingly.

4. **Warming Up:** Prioritize physical and mental warm-ups before social engagements to boost performance and confidence.

TASKS

1. **Emotional Check-In:** Reflect on your current emotional state and how it affects your social interactions. Identify recurring patterns and areas for improvement.

2. **Mood-Enhancement Routine:** Establish a personalized routine that includes sleep, healthy eating, exercise, and mental wellness practices to consistently foster a positive mood.

3. **Optimizing Surroundings:** Assess your environment and make necessary adjustments to create a positive space that encourages social engagement.

4. **Preparation Techniques:** Experiment with vocal warm-ups, reenergizing activities, mental preparation, and mood-enhancing supplements to prime your mood before social engagements.

5. **Practicing Social Interactions:** Engage in role-play exercises with friends, leverage online resources, and simulate social scenarios to build confidence and refine your social skills.

6. **Incorporating Feedback:** Seek feedback from colleagues or mentors on your emotional state and performance in social interactions. Use this feedback to modify and enhance your approach.

7. **Ongoing Improvement:** Foster a mindset of continuous improvement in managing emotions and social interactions. Remain open to learning and refining strategies for better results.

Remember, harnessing the power of emotions in social interactions requires consistent dedication and practice. By incorporating mood-enhancing strategies and actively practicing social interactions, you can improve your communication skills and establish deeper connections with others.

BODY LANGUAGE MASTERY

MASTERING BODY LANGUAGE FOR APPROACHING

WHEN YOU'RE PREPARING TO APPROACH SOMEONE, it's important to project confidence and openness. The aim here is to ensure that your vibe is inviting rather than off-putting.

Imagine yourself in a big pool of honey. Move slowly and gracefully. Avoid mechanical, sudden, and jerky movements.

Start with your feet firmly planted on the ground, symbolizing your stability and groundedness. Your shoulders should be relaxed and pulled back, avoiding any slouch that could convey defeat or insecurity. Keep your head held high and your eyes forward, displaying your self-assuredness and readiness to engage.

Your hands also play a crucial role in your approach. Avoid hiding them up to the wrists in your pockets or behind your back, as this could signal distrust or nervousness. Instead, let them hang naturally by your sides or use them to gesture as you speak, adding emphasis and expressiveness to your conversation.

Lastly, remember to respect personal space. Invading another person's personal bubble can make them feel uncomfortable and defensive. As you approach, maintain a respectful distance until the other person signals through their own body language that they're comfortable with you coming closer. For instance, they might express open body language, smile, and have their feet pointed toward you.

HOW TO COMMUNICATE THROUGH BODY LANGUAGE

Mastering your body language during the approach isn't about putting on a performance or pretending to be someone you're not—it's about presenting the best version of yourself.

Let's begin by looking at some universal successful implementations.

EYE CONTACT: WEAK VS. STRONG

Eye contact is a potent signal of confidence and interest. Averting your eyes can be misconstrued as insecurity or disinterest, while maintaining steady eye contact conveys assurance and engagement. For instance, when introducing yourself at a networking event, holding steady eye contact sets a positive and confident tone for the conversation.

ATTENTION: CONSTANTLY LOOKING AROUND VS. STAYING FOCUSED

Presence is key in any interaction. If you're habitually scanning the room or darting your eyes in different directions, it may imply that you're disinterested or uneasy. Instead, strive to stay engaged in the conversation at hand. For example, resist the temptation to glance around when chatting with a colleague at a work function. Demonstrate genuine interest in their words by maintaining focus on the conversation.

ATTENTION SEEKING: TRYING TO CATCH SOMEONE'S EYE VS. MAKING PEOPLE WORK FOR YOUR ATTENTION

While attention from high-status individuals can feel validating, incessantly seeking approval can hint at low self-esteem. Strive to hold your ground in conversations, signaling that you value your own opinions and thoughts. For example, instead of attempting to catch the eye of a senior executive at a company meeting, concentrate on offering meaningful insights to the discussion.

MOVEMENT: FIDGETING VS. STILLNESS

Stillness radiates confidence and composure, whereas fidgeting can suggest nervousness or discomfort. Aim to maintain a calm demeanor during interactions, even under stress. For instance, resist the urge to pace or play with your pen during a presentation. Stand confidently, use purposeful gestures, and actively engage with your audience.

POSTURE: COLLAPSED AND CONTRACTED BODY VS. POISED AND TAKING UP SPACE

Your posture can speak volumes about your confidence level. A poised stance—standing tall and occupying space—conveys assurance, whereas hunching or crossing your arms can suggest insecurity. To exude confidence, enter a crowded event with your shoulders back and head held high. This posture signals approachability to others and boosts your own self-assurance. Don't be afraid to take up space; unless it is very crowded, like on a subway, you have the right to take up space! Use this rule not just with your body but also with your belongings and your voice.

VOLUME: TALKING QUIETLY VS. TALKING LOUDLY

The volume of your voice can significantly impact perceptions of your confidence. Speaking too softly may suggest timidity or even come across as creepy. Speaking in close to a shouting volume can seem aggressive. Aim for a balance; articulate your words clearly and audibly without overpowering others. When introducing yourself at a social gathering, project your voice to be clearly heard, but avoid shouting over ambient noise. You can gauge the average volume of the individuals in the room and be just a decibel louder than that to give a more excitable energy. When you walk into a new environment, pay attention to the average volume of individuals and aim for a tick above that.

PACE: TALKING/MOVING
QUICKLY VS. SLOWLY

The speed at which you talk and move can influence how others perceive you. Rapid speech or movements may indicate nervousness or impatience, while slow, deliberate actions convey calmness and control. People who come across as rushing give the impression they are not used to being listened to. Act as though you're used to people being eager to hear every word you say.

Mastering these facets of body language and voice can significantly enhance your ability to approach new people successfully. Remember, practice is key, and with time, these behaviors will become an integral part of your social skills.

THE CAR ANALOGY: ADJUSTING
THE INTENSITY OF SOCIAL PRESSURE

Let's walk through the "Car Analogy," a unique approach to adjusting the intensity of social pressure during interactions.

Picture yourself as a car, where each component of the vehicle symbolizes a different element of body language. Learning how to modify these components can influence the level of social pressure exerted on the other person, thereby allowing you to navigate a spectrum of encounters, from intimate relationships to casual street encounters. By adjusting yourself and your body language, you can adjust the pressure and investment level in each interaction.

HIGH BEAMS AND LOW BEAMS: EYE CONTACT AND CHEST POSTURE

The eyes are your high beams, offering intense focus and illuminating the person you're interacting with. Your chest, on the other hand, serves as the low beam. Its position can regulate the intensity of social pressure, subtly modulating the warmth or coolness of your approach.

HIGH BEAMS

Eye contact is the high-beam setting of your headlights. This is a very strong "social spotlight" you can shine on someone. It puts social attention on the person, upping the social pressure. A good rule of thumb is to maintain eye contact 70–80% of the time when the other person is speaking and 30–70% when you are speaking, depending on the comfort level of the relationship. The less intimate the context (meeting someone walking by on the street vs. meeting your best friend at a café), the more social pressure the other person feels. So the less intimate the context, the more aware you should be of regulating this pressure.

LOW BEAMS

Your chest posture can be likened to the low beams of a car. By facing your chest toward the person, you put more attention on them; by angling away from them, you give the impression of being on the verge of walking away, thus reducing the social pressure on the other person. This strategy can be particularly useful when approaching new people or those with whom you have limited familiarity.

Let's explore different social scenarios to illuminate the application of these concepts.

EXAMPLE 1 (CLOSE RELATIONSHIP): When conversing with a close friend, comfortably open your chest, maintain direct eye contact, face forward, and lean in slightly to convey warmth and familiarity.

EXAMPLE 2 (ACQUAINTANCE): When interacting with a coworker or casual acquaintance, you might still open your chest and face them, but lean back a bit more to strike a balance between warmth and professionalism.

EXAMPLE 3 (STRANGER ON THE STREET): When approaching a stranger, slightly open your chest, lean back, and maintain a side angle (after a handshake, if appropriate). This minimizes social pressure and facilitates a more comfortable interaction.

As the conversation progresses, you can play with facing them more or less, depending on their interest indicators.

THE HORN: YOUR VOICE AND ITS IMPACT

Your voice, much like a car's horn, can significantly influence the dynamics of a conversation. Modulating your voice tone, volume, and animation can set the tone and direction of the interaction.

TONE

Adopt a warm, friendly tone to create a welcoming atmosphere and help put the other person at ease. A commanding yet respectful tone can establish your presence and authority in professional settings, and a soft, empathetic tone is often effective in sensitive or emotional discussions, fostering a space of understanding and support.

VOLUME

Adjust your volume to match the setting and the other person's comfort level. Speak louder in noisy settings and softer in more intimate ones. A great rule of thumb is to estimate the average volume of individuals in the room or group and raise yours by about one decibel. This subtle increase can make you appear more exciting and confident to listeners.

ANIMATION

Use vocal variety and expression to demonstrate enthusiasm and engage the other person in the conversation. Altering the pace, pitch, and emphasis in your speech can captivate your listener's attention and convey your emotions more effectively. Incorporating pauses strategically can add weight to your words, allowing time for reflection and emphasizing key points.

By adjusting the intensity of social pressure through your body language and voice, you can steer your social interactions with ease and confidence, creating meaningful connections along the way.

Directing all three of the car components on someone (eye contact, chest facing them, while talking) puts a lot of social pressure on the person. This can leave the other person feeling intimidated. The less intimate the context, the less pressure you should put on someone during the approach. For instance, if you're stopping a stranger on the street, you may just want to face your head toward the person and only later slowly turn toward them.

THE ART OF MIRRORING: FIND THEIR ENERGY

Mirroring is a powerful technique that involves subtly imitating another person's body language, energy, and pace of speech. This process can foster a sense of rapport and similarity, promoting a feeling of comfort and familiarity. It's often referred to as the "chameleon effect" in social psychology.

However, mirroring should be approached with caution and finesse. Overdoing it or mimicking behaviors that don't align with your personality can come across as insincere or manipulative. The key is subtlety and authenticity.

For example, if someone speaks and moves slowly and softly, adopting a similar pace can make the conversation flow more smoothly. If they use expressive hand gestures or lean forward slightly, you might mirror these actions in moderation.

While mirroring can create a sense of connection, over-reliance on this technique might inadvertently position you as a follower rather than an equal participant in the interaction. Therefore, when approaching and conversing, it's essential to strike a balance between mirroring and maintaining your autonomy and voice in the conversation. I usually recommend avoiding mirroring so you can be your natural self in the conversation. Make sure, however, not to go to the opposite extreme of their energy and movements.

PRACTICAL TIPS

Here are some key tips to help you apply these body language techniques effectively.

MAINTAIN EYE CONTACT: Practice holding eye contact for a few seconds longer than usual to show genuine interest in the conversation. Play around with the amount of eye contact you use in your conversations.

OPEN YOUR CHEST: Practice opening and facing your chest to others in various social scenarios and adjust the intensity of social pressure to create a warmer or colder approach.

LEAN BACK: Experiment with leaning back slightly to reduce social pressure and make the other person feel more at ease. You can even lean and face a direction as if you're ready to leave at any moment in colder approaches.

ADJUST YOUR STANCE ANGLE: When meeting new people, stand with them at a side angle to create a comfortable, low-pressure atmosphere. You can then slowly face them more or less, depending on comfort.

VARY YOUR VOICE: Experiment with different tones, volumes, and degrees of animation to find the most effective vocal delivery for various situations.

COMMUNICATE WISELY WITH YOUR BODY

Mastering body language techniques and adjusting the intensity of social pressure can significantly enhance your ability to communicate effectively and build meaningful connections. By following the "Car Analogy," you can navigate social interactions with ease, adjusting your body language to create warm or cold approaches based on the relationship and situation. Remember, continuous personal growth and maintaining a friendly, approachable demeanor are key to fostering genuine connections with others.

KEY INSIGHTS

1. **Displaying Confidence and Openness:** Exhibit confidence and openness through conscious body language to make your presence welcoming.

2. **Basics of Body Language:** Begin with steady footing, shoulders back, and an upright head. Ensure that your hands are visible and maintain appropriate personal space to communicate trust and ease.

3. **Effective Communication:** Mastering body language is about showcasing the best version of yourself, not putting on a performance. Use eye contact, attention, movement, posture, volume, pace, and mirroring to demonstrate confidence and interest.

4. **Adjustment of Intensity:** Comprehend the "Car Analogy" to modify the intensity of social pressure in interactions. Employ eye contact and chest posture to balance warmth and coolness in approaches.

TASKS

Your assignment this week is to apply the principles of body language and voice modulation previously discussed. Here's a detailed breakdown:

1. **Eye Contact Practice:** For the next week, consciously make an effort to maintain eye contact during conversations, whether it's with your family, friends, or colleagues. Notice how it affects the dynamic of your interactions. Try this 20 times.

2. **Attention Awareness:** During conversations, be mindful of where your attention goes. If you find yourself looking around or getting distracted, gently bring your focus back to the person you're talking to.

3. **Evaluate Attention Seeking:** Reflect on past interactions where you sought the approval of others. Try to replace this behavior by valuing your own thoughts and opinions, and focus on contributing meaningfully to conversations.

4. **Movement Observation:** Notice any fidgeting habits you have, like tapping your foot or clicking a pen. Make a conscious effort to reduce these behaviors and maintain a calm demeanor during interactions.

5. **Posture Awareness:** Work on improving your posture this week. Each day, spend a few minutes practicing standing tall and taking up space. Notice how it makes you feel and how others respond to you.

6. **Volume Control:** Experiment with the volume of your voice in different settings—at home, at work, and in social gatherings. Find your "Goldilocks zone" where your voice is neither too loud nor too soft.

7. **Pace Yourself:** Pay attention to the pace of your speech and movements. If you catch yourself rushing, slow down. Practice speaking slowly and deliberately, especially when explaining complex topics.

Remember, these tasks are about building awareness and making gradual improvements. Don't expect overnight changes. Instead, focus on small wins and consistent progress.

MAKE YOUR APPROACH

REACHING THE CONCLUSION OF THIS GUIDE MARKS NOT THE END but rather the beginning of a new chapter in your social journey, equipped with insights and strategies for effective communication.

Throughout this book, we've delved into the nuances of initiating social interactions, unraveling the complexities of the Direct and Indirect Approaches. We've explored how to create meaningful first impressions, manage social anxiety, and use our surroundings to our advantage. We've emphasized the significance of grooming, fashion, and mood in setting the stage for positive interactions.

The art of approaching someone may seem daunting at first, but it's a skill that can be honed with practice and patience. The strategies and insights shared in these pages are more than just techniques; they're stepping stones toward building confidence and enhancing your social repertoire.

Remember, the first 10 seconds of an interaction set the tone for what follows. Whether it's a simple compliment, a shared interest, or a keen observation, your approach is the key to unlocking a world of social possibilities. By mastering this art, you open doors to new friendships, professional networks, and enriching conversations.

As you move forward, keep in mind that every approach is unique. What works in one situation may not be as effective in another. It's about being adaptable, observant, and genuine. Your authenticity in these moments is what truly resonates with people.

Finally, I encourage you to continue your journey at Jaunty.org. There is so much more to discover, whether you're interested in building confidence, overcoming social anxiety, furthering relationships, or simply developing your interpersonal skills. Our community is a vibrant space for practicing, sharing, and evolving your social acumen with real people. You'll find support, camaraderie, and endless opportunities to apply what you've learned in real-world settings.

The Approach is not just a book—it's a gateway to a more socially fulfilling life. As we close this chapter, remember that the art of saying hello is just the beginning. Your journey toward social mastery and meaningful connections is an ongoing adventure, one you are now well-equipped to embark upon.

REFERENCES & ENDNOTES

Ambady, N., Bernieri, F. J., & Richeson, J. A. (2000). Toward a histology of social behavior: Judgmental accuracy from thin slices of the behavioral stream. *Advances in Experimental Social Psychology*, 32, 201–271.

Bales, R. F. (1950). *Interaction process analysis: A method for the study of small groups.* Addison-Wesley.

Forgas, J. P. (1998). On feeling good and getting your way: Mood effects on negotiator cognition and bargaining strategies. Journal of Personality and Social Psychology.

Hofmann, S. G., Asnaani, A., & Hinton, D. E. (2010). Cultural aspects in social anxiety and social anxiety disorder. *Depression and Anxiety.*

Kellermann, K. (1984). The negativity effect and its implications for initial interaction. *Communication Monographs*, 51(1), 37–55.

Martin, R. A., Puhlik-Doris, P., Larsen, G., Gray, J., & Weir, K. (2003). Individual differences in uses of humor and their relation to psychological well-being: Development of the Humor Styles Questionnaire. *Journal of Research in Personality, 37*(1), 48–75.

Naumann, L. P., Vazire, S., Rentfrow, P. J., & Gosling, S. D. (2009). Personality judgments based on physical appearance. *Personality and Social Psychology Bulletin.*

Rogers, C. R. (1961). *On becoming a person: A therapist's view of psychotherapy.* Houghton Mifflin.

Willis, J., & Todorov, A. (2006). First impressions: Making up your mind after a 100-ms exposure to a face. *Psychological Science, 17*(7), 592–598.

ENDNOTES

THE POWER OF HUMOR

1. Research has shown that humor can play a significant role in social interactions by reducing tension and fostering a sense of connection. For example, a study by Martin et al. (2003) found that humor can enhance perceptions of sociability and competence in social settings.

AUTHENTICITY IS KEY

2. Authenticity in social interactions is supported by the work of psychologists such as Rogers (1961), who emphasized the importance of being genuine in forming meaningful connections with others.

THE DIRECT APPROACH

3. The effectiveness of direct communication in social interactions is supported by research on interpersonal communication. For instance, a study by Kellermann (1984) suggests that directness can lead to more successful communication outcomes.

BREAKING DOWN THE DIRECT APPROACH

4. The importance of a warm greeting is supported by research on first impressions, such as the work by Willis and Todorov (2006), which indicates that initial interactions can significantly impact the development of interpersonal relationships.

STRATEGIES FOR APPROACHING A GROUP

5. The strategy of waiting for the right moment to approach a group aligns with findings on group dynamics and social entry, as discussed in research by Bales (1950) on interaction process analysis.

THE INDIRECT APPROACH

6. The use of subtlety in the Indirect Approach can be linked to the concept of implicit communication in social psychology, as explored by Ambady et al. (1992) in their research on thin slices of behavior and the accuracy of social judgments.

OVERCOMING SOCIAL ANXIETY

7. Hofmann, Asnaani, and Hinton (2010) discuss cognitive-behavioral therapy (CBT) techniques for managing social anxiety, highlighting the effectiveness of exposure and cognitive restructuring.

FIRST IMPRESSIONS AND NONVERBAL CUES

8. Naumann et al. (2009) on the effects of clothing on first impressions suggest that what one wears significantly influences others' perceptions of their personality, status, and competence.

MOOD AND SOCIAL INTERACTION

9. Forgas (1998) demonstrates how mood can influence social behavior, including memory, judgment, and interpersonal strategies.

Made in the USA
Monee, IL
15 October 2024

68094299R00067